CHRISTIANITY|EXPLORED

WHAT'S THE BEST NEWS
YOU'VE EVER HEARD?

JESUS' Call

HANDBOOK

Christianity Explored Handbook (4th Edition)
Copyright © Christianity Explored 2016. Reprinted 2017
www.christianityexplored.org

Published by:
The Good Book Company Ltd
Blenheim House, 1 Blenheim Road, Epsom, Surrey, KT19 9AP, UK
Tel: 0333 123 0880; International: +44 (0) 208 942 0880
Email: info@thegoodbook.com

Websites:
North America: www.thegoodbook.com
UK and Europe: www.thegoodbook.co.uk
Australia: www.thegoodbook.com.au
New Zealand: www.thegoodbook.co.nz

ISBN: 9781784980771

Design by André Parker

Printed in India

CONTENTS

WELCOME TO CHRISTIANITY|EXPLORED

Over the next seven sessions we will explore three questions that cut right to the heart of Christianity: Who is Jesus? What did he achieve? How should we respond?

Don't be afraid to ask questions, no matter how simple or difficult you think they are. And if you have to miss a week, don't worry. There is a short summary of the previous session at the start of the next one.

SESSION 1
GOOD NEWS

◎ EXPLORE

What's the best news you've ever heard?

JESUS' Calling ME...

🎙 **LISTEN**

"The beginning of the gospel about Jesus Christ..."
(Mark 1:1)

- When we see the order and beauty of the world and the human body, the question is: Did this all happen by chance? Or did someone create it?

- The Bible says God is the One who created the universe we live in and the bodies we inhabit. So how can we know him?

- We can know what God is like by looking at Jesus Christ.

- Christianity is about Christ – a title that means "God's only chosen King".

- Christianity is the "gospel" – "the good news" – about Jesus Christ.

- When Jesus was baptized, God the Father announced, "You are my Son".

- God has revealed himself in human history through Jesus Christ. When we look at Jesus, all the guessing games about God stop. AMEN

⊜ DISCUSS

1. Is there anything that intrigues or puzzles you about Jesus?

2. How do you feel about reading Mark's Gospel?

3. If you could ask God one question, and you knew it would
   be answered, what would it be?

   Take me to heaven!
   Teach me!

Bible words

Gospel: Good news.
Christ/Messiah: God's only chosen King, whom God promised to send into the world.
Prophet: God's messenger.
Baptism: Immersion in water as a symbol of turning from sin and being washed clean on the inside.

Repentance: A change of mind and purpose. Personally turning back to God.
Holy Spirit: There is one God in three Persons: God the Father, God the Son (that's Jesus) and God the Holy Spirit.

[handwritten top margin: "Monday" ... "Jody" "those in pain..." "Moore" "Cathy husband"]

→ FOLLOW UP

Each week you'll be exploring a few chapters of Mark. By the
end of Session 6, you'll have read the whole of Mark's Gospel.
Use the following questions to help you explore the passage.
There's room at the end to write down any questions you'd like
to discuss next time.

Read Mark 1:1-20

1. The word "gospel" means "good news". Mark begins his
   book of good news with three statements about Jesus:

   a) by the Old Testament prophets (messengers) (Mark 1:2-3)
   b) by John the Baptist (Mark 1:7)
   c) by God himself (Mark 1:11)

   ☆ What do they each say about Jesus?

[handwritten left margin: "Trinity", "Voice from", "Spirit -", "Son himself", "Ezekiel sp?", "Essency"]

[handwritten answers:]

a) Isaiah "Be prepared for" the Voice crying in the wilderness. Be prepared for the of the LORD"

[left margin: ".700 yrs before CHRIST...", "Jews had to do a furry Around to be baptised, people wanted to be Jew - H.S. if they"]

b) John v7 "After He comes, one Mightier than I, HE will Baptise you w/ the HOLY SPIRIT"

c) Mark 1-11 "you are my BELOVED SON, w/ of GOD whom I am well pleased"

Tuesday

Read Mark 1:21 – 2:17

2. In chapters 1 and 2 Jesus shows his authority in different
situations. (See Mark 1:16-20, 21-22, 23-28, 40-45; 2:1-12.)
When Jesus speaks or acts, what sorts of things happen?

√21-27 Even the unclean spirit recognizes JESUS.
V29 - JESUS heals the sick.
√38 - They went to the next Towns. As we went
He preached + cast out demons ———

Also forgives SIN.

Read Mark 2:18 – 3:6

3. Even at this early stage, Jesus divided opinions. Some
people were amazed by him, while others were enraged.
What are your early impressions of Jesus?

I wish I was there to see JESUS in the
beginning.
He did not placate the people. They would have to
discover who JESUS
3:4-5   was for themselves

Do you have any questions about Mark 1:1 – 3:6?

SESSION 2
IDENTITY

⬅ SUMMARY

In the last session we saw that Christianity is about Christ. It is the good news (the "gospel") about Jesus Christ. You can see a short summary of last session's talk/video on page 8. In this session we will see what Mark tells us about who Jesus is,

◎ EXPLORE

- *Discuss any questions from last session's Follow Up.*

- *Look together at Mark 1:35-11 and answer the questions below.*

1. What hope of surviving the storm did the disciples have?

Very little, no faith — YET

2. What is so remarkable about the way in which Jesus calms the storm? (See Mark 4:39.)

JESUS spoke CALMLY. AND in FAith Apostle still havent collected the gift of the H.S. = FAith

3. The verses below (from Psalm 107) were a familiar song praising God for his power over the sea. The disciples would have known it well. As you read it, look for similarities with their experience in Mark 4:35-41.

> 23 *Others went out on the sea in ships;*
> *they were merchants on the mighty waters.*
> 24 *They saw the works of the LORD,*
> *his wonderful deeds in the deep.*
> 25 *For he spoke and stirred up a tempest*
> *that lifted high the waves.*
> 26 *They mounted up to the heavens and went down to the depths;*
> *in their peril their courage melted away.*
> 27 *They reeled and staggered like drunken men;*
> *they were at their wits' end.*
> 28 *Then they cried out to the LORD in their trouble,*
> *and he brought them out of their distress.*
> 29 *He stilled the storm to a whisper;*
> *the waves of the sea were hushed.*

30 They were glad when it grew calm,
   and he guided them to their desired haven.
31 Let them give thanks to the LORD for his (un)failing love
   and his wonderful deeds for men.

Psalm 107:23-31

What similarities did you notice?

*The Song tells the Story
in the Bibles words*

4. The song and the story end in two different ways. (See Psalm
   107:30 and Mark 4:41.) Why were the disciples still terrified
   after the storm had been calmed?

*Mark 4:41 - they learn of JESUS
who HE really is...*

*Psalm 107:30 - the Apostles accepted
CHRIST authority greatfully*

*C.GC Greatfully learning the Gift
of CHRIST's Teaching... V28*

◉))) LISTEN

"Who is this? Even the wind and the waves obey him!"
(Mark 4:41)

- It's important to get the identity of Jesus right – otherwise we'll relate to him in the wrong way.

- Mark reveals the identity of Jesus by showing:

  1. his power and authority to teach (Mark 1:21-22).
  2. his power and authority over sickness (Mark 1:29-31, 32-34, 3:22).
  3. his power and authority over nature (Mark 4:35-41; see also Psalm 107:23-31).
  4. his power and authority over death (Mark 5:21-24, 35-43).
  5. his power and authority to forgive sin (Mark 2:1-12).

- As God's Son and God's only chosen King, Jesus behaves with God's authority and displays God's power.

💬 DISCUSS

1. What do you think of the evidence Mark gives us?

True & Worthy
Mark saw JESUS in action
Apostles saw for themselves

2. What is your view of who Jesus is?

GOD made himself human
in CHRIST who had power & Authority
P16

Bible words

Disciples: Those called to follow Jesus, learn from him and be witnesses of his ministry.
Sabbath: The Jewish day set aside for rest and enjoyment of God.
Sins: Rebellion against God. Failure to think, say and do what we should.
Blaspheming: Misrepresenting God, or treating his name and character carelessly.
Son of Man: This title comes from the Old Testament book of Daniel, where the Son of Man came from heaven and was given eternal rule over the whole world. Jesus often used this title for himself.

⊖→ FOLLOW UP

Each week you'll be exploring a few chapters of Mark. By the end of Session 6, you'll have read the whole of Mark's Gospel. Use the following questions to help you explore the passage. There's room at the end to write down any questions you'd like to discuss next time.

Read Mark 3:7 – 5:43

1. In this passage Mark records Jesus doing four specific miracles:

   a) calming a storm (Mark 4:35-41)
   b) healing a demon-possessed man (Mark 5:1-20)
   c) healing a sick woman (Mark 5:25-34)
   d) raising a dead girl to life (Mark 5:35-43

   What does Jesus show authority over in these events?

   a)

   b)

   c)

   d)

• How does this add to what we've already seen about his power and authority in the earlier chapters?

2. When Jairus' daughter died, and all hope seemed to be lost (Mark 5:35), what did Jesus ask Jairus to do (verse 36)?

• Was that a "reasonable" thing to ask?

3. Looking at all four events (see question 1), what are the different ways in which people respond to Jesus? See...

a) Mark 4:40-41

b) Mark 5:15

c) Mark 5:27-28, 34

d) Mark 5:42

• Do you see yourself in any of these responses?

Do you have any questions about Mark 3:7 – 5:43?

SESSION 3

SIN

← **SUMMARY**

In the last session we saw that Jesus is the Christ (God's only chosen King) and God's Son. You can see a short summary of last session's talk/video on page 16. In this session we will see what Mark tells us about why Jesus came.

◎ **EXPLORE**

- *Discuss any questions from last session's Follow Up.*

- *Look together at Mark 2:1-12 and answer the questions below.*

1. A huge crowd had gathered to hear Jesus. Why?
   What kind of reputation had he built up in these early days?
   (Look at Mark 1:27-28, 32-34, 45 for clues.)

2. What were the four men hoping Jesus would do?

3. What does Jesus do instead in Mark 2:5? Why do you think he does this first of all?

4. Why were the teachers of the law so annoyed by what Jesus said? (See Mark 2:6-7.)

5. Had they reached the right conclusion?

6. How do we know that Jesus has authority to forgive sin? (See Mark 2:8-12.) Good for explaining CHRIST to the lost

))) LISTEN

"I have not come to call the righteous, but sinners."

(Mark 2:17)

- The reason the world is not the way it's supposed to be is because we are not the way we're supposed to be.

- Jesus tells us that "sin" comes "from within", from our "hearts" (Mark 7:20-22).

- Each of us has a heart problem. We often treat each other and our world in a shameful way, and we treat God in that way too.

- We should love God with all our heart, soul, mind and strength. But we never manage to do this.

- We've all rebelled against God, our loving Creator. The Bible calls this "sin".

- Jesus came to cure our heart problem, the problem of our sin. He came for people who realize they're bad, not for people who think they're good.

- Jesus lovingly warns us about hell because he does not want us to go there. Our sin means we're all in danger, whether we realize it or not (Mark 9:43-47).

Hyperbole

⬅ DISCUSS

1. Read Mark 9:43-47. Why do you think Jesus used such extreme language when talking about the need to avoid hell?

2. Jesus believed in hell. Should we? Why or why not?

3. Imagine that all of your thoughts, words and actions were displayed for everyone to see. How would you feel?

Bible words

Soul: The part of us that lives for ever.
Sinners: Those who sin (which is all of us). See "sins" on page 17.

Pharisees: Jewish religious leaders.
Righteous: Being right with God.

→ **FOLLOW UP**

Use the following questions to help you explore the passage. There's room at the end to write down any questions you'd like to discuss next time.

Read Mark 6:1 – 8:29

1. In the earlier chapters (1 – 5) Mark has built up a picture of Jesus' power and authority. He's shown us various miracles: healing the sick, casting out demons, raising the dead, calming a storm.

   How does this passage (Mark 6:1 – 8:29) add to that picture? (See Mark 6:32-44, 47-48; 7:31-37; 8:1-10, 22-26.)

2. Jesus saw the large crowd in Mark 6:34 as "sheep without a shepherd". What did he do about it?

   • If Jesus looked at the faces of people in a busy town today, do you think he would feel the same? Why / why not?

• Do you feel the need to have Jesus as your shepherd?

3. Write down the very different reactions to Jesus' preaching and miracles:

a) in his home synagogue (Mark 6:1-6).

b) among people generally (Mark 6:14-15, 53-56; 7:37).

c) from the disciples (Mark 6:51-52).

d) from the religious leaders (Mark 8:11).

• Why do you think people responded so differently in each of these cases?

- Do you identify particularly with one of those groups?

4. Read Jesus' question in Mark 8:29. How would you have answered this before you started *Christianity Explored*?

- Now that you're halfway through Mark's Gospel, and have read about the amazing things that Jesus said and did, has your answer changed?

- If you still have questions about the identity of Jesus, write them below.

Do you have any questions about Mark 6:1 – 8:29?

SESSION 4
THE CROSS

⟵ SUMMARY

In the last session we saw that Jesus came to cure our heart problem – our sin. You can see a short summary of last session's talk/video on page 24. In this session we will see what Mark tells us about why Jesus died.

⊙ EXPLORE

- *Discuss any questions from last session's Follow Up.*

- *Look together at Mark 8:22-33 and answer the questions below.*

1. Generally speaking, who do people today believe Jesus is? What do they base these views on?

2. Peter's statement in Mark 8:29 seems to form a turning point in Mark's Gospel (see Mark 8:31).

   What did Peter say, and why do you think it was so important?

3. Once the identity of Jesus was clear (Mark 8:29), he went on to explain his mission in Mark 8:31-32. Why do you think Peter rebuked Jesus? (See Mark 8:32-33.)

4. Mark records the two-stage healing of the blind man in Mark 8:22-26. The healing process took the blind man from seeing nothing (Mark 8:22) to seeing something (Mark 8:24) to seeing everything (Mark 8:25). How clearly are the disciples "seeing" the identity and mission of Jesus in Mark 8:27-33?

5. Jesus told Peter he had in mind "the things of men". What phrase did Jesus use to describe his suffering and death (Mark 8:33)?

• What does this tell us about his mission?

6. In Mark 8:29, Jesus asks: "But what about you? Who do you say I am?" Are you able to give a definite answer to this question yet? If so, how would you answer and why?

Bible words

Satan: A spiritual being whose name means "adversary". He is the adversary of God, his people, and all that is good. He is also called the devil.

Ransom: A price paid so that a slave could be set free.

LISTEN

"For even the Son of Man did not come to be served, but to serve, and to give his life as a ransom for many."
(Mark 10:45)

- Jesus' death on a cross wasn't a tragic waste of life. It was a rescue.
- Jesus taught his followers that he must be killed. He came to "give his life as a ransom for many" (Mark 10:45).
- As Jesus was dying on the cross, darkness came over the whole land. God was acting in anger to punish sin.
- On the cross, Jesus was in some way "forsaken" or abandoned by God, as God punished sin.
- Jesus gave himself up as a substitute, to be punished on our behalf. He bore the punishment that our sin deserves, so that we can be rescued.
- When Jesus died, the curtain in the temple was torn in two from top to bottom (Mark 15:38). Because of the cross, the way is now open for people to approach God.

- The people who saw Jesus die reacted in different ways:

  - The soldiers missed what was happening.
  - The religious leaders were convinced they already knew the way to God.
  - The Roman governor, Pontius Pilate, gave in to the crowd.
  - The Roman centurion recognized the identity of Jesus: "Surely this man was the Son of God!" (Mark 15:39).

⬚ DISCUSS

1. How would you feel if someone else deliberately took the punishment for something serious you had done wrong?

2. Which of the reactions to Jesus' death is most like your reaction?

3. Jesus said he came "to give his life as a ransom" for sinners (Mark 10:45). What will you do with your sin?

⊖ FOLLOW UP

Use the following questions to help you explore the passage. There's room at the end to write down any questions you'd like to discuss next time.

Read Mark 8:30 – 10:52

(Note that "Son of Man" is Jesus' way of referring to himself.)

1. Jesus directly predicts his own death and resurrection three times (Mark 8:31, 9:31 and 10:33-34). What does he say "must" and "will" happen?

2. In Mark 8:31 Jesus said he "must" die. Why did he have to die? (See Mark 10:45.)

3. What did Jesus say that following him would mean? (See Mark 8:34.)

4. Each time Jesus predicts his own death and resurrection, Mark records the disciples' response – or lack of it. (See Mark 8:32-33; 9:33-35; 10:35-45.) How do the disciples respond in each case?

a) Mark 8:32-33

b) Mark 9:32-35

c) Mark 10:35-41

5. In Mark 8:29 Peter recognizes that Jesus is the Christ, God's only chosen King. In taking Jesus aside and rebuking him (Mark 8:32), Peter is not treating Jesus as God's King. How do you think you have treated Jesus?

• How would you feel about Jesus being King in every area of your life?

Do you have any questions about Mark 8:30 – 10:52?

SESSION 5
RESURRECTION

⟵ SUMMARY

In the last session we saw that Jesus died to rescue us from sin, by taking the punishment we deserve. You can see a short summary of last session's talk/video on page 32. In this session we will see what Mark tells us about why Jesus rose from the dead.

◎ EXPLORE

- *Discuss any questions from last session's Follow Up.*

- *Look together at Mark 14:27-31 and answer the questions below.*

1. In this section Jesus is speaking to his disciples. What predictions did Jesus make? (See Mark 14:27, 28 and 30.)

2. In what ways does Peter disagree with Jesus' predictions? (See Mark 14:29, 31.)

3. In Mark 14:27 Jesus quoted from the Old Testament (Zechariah 13:7) to explain what he was about to suffer, and why the disciples would scatter.

   How do we know that Jesus fully intended to gather the "sheep" who would be scattered by his death? (See Mark 14:28 and Mark 16:6-7.)

4. Which of Jesus' predictions did Peter pay attention to?

• Which did he ignore?

5. Jesus had spoken plainly and repeatedly about his resurrection from death. (See Mark 8:31, 9:30-31, 10:32-34.) Did the disciples understand what this meant? If not, why didn't they ask Jesus about it? (See Mark 9:32.)

Bible words

Gentiles: Non-Jews.
Pilate: Roman governor in Jerusalem.

Kingdom of God: Wherever God's King (Jesus) rules over God's people. Not a geographical kingdom.

41

⊙ LISTEN

"He has risen! ... just as he told you."
(Mark 16:6-7)

- Jesus repeatedly claimed that he would be raised to life on the third day after his death.

- Jesus really did die: the women, Joseph of Arimathea, the Roman centurion and Pontius Pilate were all certain that Jesus had died.

- 36 hours later, the huge, heavy stone covering the entrance to his tomb had been rolled away.

- A young man in a white robe told the women that Jesus had risen from death. He also said that the disciples would see Jesus in Galilee, just as he had told them before he died.

- Jesus appeared to his disciples on at least ten separate occasions after his death. He also appeared to more than 500 people at the same time.

- It is not only the disciples who will see the risen Jesus. We will see him too.

- The resurrection guarantees that one day we will all be physically raised from the dead. And Jesus will be our Judge on that day.

- Jesus died to pay for sin, and rose from death to prove that sin was truly paid for. If we put our trust in Jesus, all of our sin will be fully and finally forgiven.

- Because of the resurrection, we can trust Jesus with our own death. Are we ready to meet him?

DISCUSS

1. *"For God has set a day when he will judge the world with justice by the man he has appointed. He has given proof of this to all men by raising him from the dead"* (Acts 17:31). What's your reaction to this?

2. Do you believe Jesus rose from the dead? Why or why not?

⊕ FOLLOW UP

Use the following questions to help you explore the passage. There's room at the end to write down any questions you'd like to discuss next time.

Read Mark 11:1-33

1. What is the crowd's attitude towards Jesus as he arrives in Jerusalem? (See Mark 11:8-10.)

2. The Old Testament prophet Zechariah wrote about a time when someone would ride into Jerusalem (also called Zion) on a colt.

> *Rejoice greatly, O Daughter of Zion!*
> *Shout, Daughter of Jerusalem!*
> *See, your king comes to you,*
> *righteous and having salvation,*
> *gentle and riding on a donkey,*
> *on a colt, the foal of a donkey.*
>
> Zechariah 9:9

What would the crowd understand about Jesus when he arrived in that way?

SESSION 5 | **RESURRECTION**

Read Mark 12:1 – 13:37

3. How do the religious leaders respond to Jesus in Mark 11:18 and 12:12?

4. How do these leaders treat Jesus as a result of their fear of him? (See Mark 11:27-33; 12:13-17.)

5. The Sadducees were a group of religious leaders who did not believe in resurrection. In Mark 12:18-23 they tried to make Jesus look foolish with their question about the resurrection. What did Jesus say was the real reason for their disbelief? (See Mark 12:24.)

45

6. What other criticism does Jesus make of religious leaders? (See Mark 12:38-40.)

7. A few days later the mood of the crowd had turned. Led by their religious leaders they demanded the death of Jesus (see Mark 15:9-13). Does it surprise you that it is possible to be respected, even religious, and still reject Jesus? Why or why not?

Do you have any questions about Mark 11:1 – 13:37?

SESSION 6
GRACE

⬅ SUMMARY

In the last session we saw that the resurrection proves that God accepted the ransom Jesus paid, that death has been beaten, and that Jesus will come back to judge everyone. You can see a short summary of last session's talk/video on page 42. In this session we will see what Mark tells us about how God can accept us because of Jesus.

⊙ EXPLORE

- *Discuss any questions from last session's Follow Up.*

- *Look together at Mark 10:13-16 and answer the questions below.*

1. From all we have seen of Jesus, why do you think people would bring their children to him? (See Mark 10:13 and 16.)

2. We are not told why the disciples rebuked those who brought their children to Jesus. What might have been the reason for their intolerance? (See Mark 9:33-34.)

3. Read Mark 9:33-37. In Mark 10:14 we are told that Jesus was indignant with the disciples. Are you surprised that he reacted so strongly? Why or why not?

4. Read Mark 10:14-15. How do we know that Jesus is not just talking about actual children belonging to the kingdom of God?

5. Read Mark 10:16. The little children did nothing to earn acceptance by Jesus. All they did was come to him and he took them in his arms. What is the significance of this for our entry into God's kingdom? (See Mark 10:15.)

◁|)) LISTEN

> *"I tell you the truth, anyone who will not receive the*
> *kingdom of God like a little child will never enter it."*
>
> (Mark 10:15)

- If God asked, "Why should I give you eternal life?", what would you say?

- The rich young man wanted to know how to be good enough for God.

- We can never do enough to inherit eternal life.

- Nothing we do can cure our heart problem.

- But we can receive eternal life as a free gift – paid for by the death of Jesus. This is grace – God's undeserved gift to us.

- We are more sinful than we ever realized, but more loved than we ever dreamed.

Bible words

Kingdom of God: Wherever God's King (Jesus) rules over God's people. Not a geographical kingdom.

Eternal life: Life in all its fullness, with God for ever in his kingdom.

DISCUSS

1. "What must I do to inherit eternal life?" (Mark 10:17)
   How would you answer that question?

2. "You are more sinful than you ever realized, but more loved
   than you ever dreamed." How do you respond to this?

3. Has grace made a difference to the view of God you had in
   Session 1?

⊕→ **FOLLOW UP**

Use the following questions to help you explore the passage. There's room at the end for you to write down any questions you'd like to discuss next time.

Read Mark 14:1-72

1. Mark tells us about Jesus' last night with his disciples, and his trial by the Jewish court, the Sanhedrin. How do we know from Mark's account that Jesus' death was not a mistake or accident? (See Mark 14:12-26, 27-31, 48-49, 61-62.)

   a) Mark 14:12-26

   b) Mark 14:27-31

   c) Mark 14:48-49

   d) Mark 14:61-62

2. Jesus knew that it was his mission to die. Does that mean that death was easy for him? (See Mark 14:33-36; 15:34.)

Read Mark 15:1 – 16:8

3. At the moment that Jesus died, something happened in the temple on the other side of the city (Mark 15:38). What happened?

- The temple curtain was like a big "No entry" sign. It showed that people were cut off from God because of their sins. Why do you think Mark records what happened to this curtain?

4. In Mark 14:50 we see the disciples deserting Jesus. In Mark 14:66-72 we see Peter repeatedly disowning him. Given all that Jesus had said about his death, why do you think they responded like this?

5. A Roman centurion was in charge of the crucifixion. What did he say when Jesus died (Mark 15:39)?

   • Why did he say this – and why is it surprising?

6. Grace is when God treats us in the opposite way to what we deserve. It is an undeserved gift. Peter had disowned Jesus three times (Mark 14:66-72). How do you think Peter would have felt when he was given the message of Mark 16:7? Why?

- The grace Jesus shows to Peter is a picture of the grace now offered to us. How will you respond to the gift Jesus offers?

Do you have any questions about Mark 14:1 – 16:8?

DAY AWAY 1
THE SOWER

← SUMMARY

In the last session we saw that God accepts us not because of anything we have done but because of what Jesus has done. This is grace – God's undeserved gift to us. You can see a short summary of last session's talk/video on page 49. During our day away we will see what it means to listen carefully, ask humbly and choose wisely.

⊙ EXPLORE

- *Look together at Mark 4:1-9 and 13-20. Answer the questions below.*

1. A parable is a story with a deeper, sometimes hidden, meaning. What does each part of this parable represent? (See Mark 4:13-20.)

   - The farmer represents…

   - The seed is…

- The path is like people who…

- The rocky soil is like those who…

- What are the thorns in real life?

- How would you recognize those who are good soil?

⟨⟩ LISTEN

> *"Then Jesus said, 'He who has ears to hear, let him hear.'"* (Mark 4:9)

- The good news about Jesus will only change your life if you hear it properly.

- The parable explains what can happen once the good news has been heard.

  1. Satan is like a thief who wants to take the gospel message from you.
  2. Some people give up on Jesus rather than put up with the cost of following him.

3. Some let their desire for other things become stronger than their desire for Jesus.
4. Some understand that Jesus is the greatest treasure in the world.

- The gospel message has the power to break through any human heart, if we will listen and act on what we hear.

🗨 DISCUSS

1. As you look back over the course, do you think some of the word has been taken from you?

2. Which type of soil would you say best describes you?

Bible words

Parable: A simple story with a spiritual meaning.

DAY AWAY 2

JAMES AND JOHN

))) LISTEN

"What do you want me to do for you?" (Mark 10:36)

- If God said, "What do you want me to do for you?", what would you ask for?

- James and John wanted power and prestige but Jesus offers something far more valuable – himself.

- Following Jesus is about service, not status.

- Contentment, satisfaction and fulfilment don't come from status-seeking, or anything else – they come from God.

- We make these things more important than God. The Bible calls this idolatry – turning something God has created into a substitute for God.

- Bartimaeus called Jesus "Son of David" and asked for mercy. He received it, and followed Jesus.

- What do you want Jesus to do for you?

⊜ DISCUSS

1. Who do you identify with most and why? James and John?
   Or Bartimaeus?

2. What do you want Jesus to do for you?

Bible words

Glory: A highly exalted state or position.   **Rabbi:** A Jewish teacher.

DAY AWAY 3
HEROD

◁|◁ **LISTEN**

> *"The king was greatly distressed, but because of his oaths and his dinner guests, he did not want to refuse her."*
>
> (Mark 6:26)

- We are the choices we have made.

- King Herod had John the Baptist put in prison.

- He liked to listen to John, but would not repent.

- Herod didn't act on what John said about Herodias. So in the end he felt forced to do something he didn't want to do – and had John killed.

- If we listen to Jesus, and take his words seriously, our family or friends may reject us. But there is a loving family of fellow believers who will support and encourage us.

- Though following Jesus will bring persecutions of one kind or another, Jesus promises that with them will come extraordinary blessings and joy.

- Ignoring Jesus' call to repent and believe may give us the approval of other people – but it will eventually earn us the rejection of Jesus.

DISCUSS

1. How do you think Herod felt about killing John the Baptist? (See Mark 6:20, 26, and then Mark 6:16.)

2. Mark tells us that "the opportune time came" (Mark 6:21). What opportunity did Herodias take? (See Mark 6:19, 24.)

3. What opportunity did Herod miss, and why?

4. What kind of soil is Herod? (See Mark 4:15-20.)

5. An old saying says, "We are the choices we have made".
   How was that true for Herod?

6. What choices will you make about the things you have heard
   during *Christianity Explored*?

SESSION 7
COME AND DIE

← SUMMARY

During the day away we saw why we need to listen carefully to God's word, ask humbly for mercy, and choose wisely how we will respond to Jesus. You can see a short summary of the talks/videos on pages 56, 59 and 61. In this closing session we will consider what it means to follow Jesus.

⊙ EXPLORE

- *Discuss any questions from last week's Follow Up.*

- *Look together at Mark 1:14-15 and answer the questions below.*

1. All through *Christianity Explored* we have heard about the good news. In Mark 1:14-15 it's mentioned twice. But to understand the good news, we need to understand the "bad news" first.

   What is the "bad news" in the following verses?

   a) Mark 7:20-23

b) Mark 9:43-47

c) Mark 10:26-27

2. *"Jesus went ... proclaiming the good news"* (Mark 1:14).
   What is the "good news" answer to these questions from the
   course?

   • Why did Jesus come?

   • Why did Jesus die?

- Why did Jesus rise?

- How can God accept us?

3. "Repent and believe the good news!" (Mark 1:15)
   To "repent" means to turn back in the opposite direction
   to the one you were travelling in. And to "believe the good
   news" means to act upon it, to build your life upon it.
   What would that mean for you?

◉))) LISTEN

> *"If anyone would come after me, he must deny himself and take up his cross and follow me."*
>
> (Mark 8:34)

- The disciples saw Jesus' power and authority – but still asked, "Who is this?"

- Jesus healed a blind man gradually.

- The gradual healing of the man's sight reflects the gradual growth of the disciples' understanding.

- Peter sees that Jesus is the Christ, God's only chosen King.

- But the disciples' "sight" is not fully healed. Although they see who Jesus is, they don't yet see why he has come or what it means to follow him.

- Following Jesus means denying self, and taking up our cross.

- If we want to save our lives, we must entrust them to Jesus.

- A true follower of Christ is someone who clearly sees what it will cost to follow him – but does it joyfully anyway, knowing that Jesus is worth infinitely more.

- What do you see when you look at:

    – Jesus' **identity**? (Is he just a good man, or is he the Christ, the Son of God?)
    – Jesus' **mission**? (Is his death a tragic waste, or is it a rescue – a "ransom for many"?)
    – Jesus' **call**? (Is it a way of losing your life, or a way of gaining it?)

DISCUSS

1. "What good is it for a man to gain the whole world, yet forfeit his soul?" (Mark 8:36) How would you answer that question?

2. How might you be ashamed of Jesus and his words (Mark 8:38)?

3. How would you score the following statements?
   (0 = completely unconvinced, 10 = very sure)

Jesus is the Christ, the Son of God.

0   10
_____

Jesus came to rescue me from my sin.

0   10
_____

Following Jesus means denying myself and putting Jesus first, whatever the cost.

0   10
_____

⊖ WHAT NOW?

"'The time has come,' he said. 'The kingdom of God is near. Repent and believe the good news!'"

(Mark 1:15)

CAN WE RELY ON
MARK'S GOSPEL?

Who? When? Why?

Mark was a close friend and companion of Peter, who was one of Jesus' disciples. Peter was an "apostle" (one of those specifically called to witness the life, death and resurrection of Jesus). Peter wrote two letters to the first-century Christian churches. In one of them he said, "I will make every effort to see that after my departure (i.e. his death) you will always remember these things" (2 Peter 1:15). He was referring to the things he saw and knew about Jesus. He passed them on to others like Mark. Peter died in the mid 60s of the 1st century. The evidence suggests that Mark wrote his Gospel around that period.

No doubt Mark was influenced by Peter's desire for the news about Jesus to be told to others in later generations, so he wrote it down in a book. His opening sentence reveals the subject of his book: "The beginning of the gospel about Jesus Christ, the Son of God" (Mark 1:1).

Jesus died, rose again and returned to heaven around AD 30. Mark wrote about 30 years later – well within the lifetime of those who lived through the events he recorded. So Mark had to write accurately. Any inconsistencies between what people saw and what he wrote would have discredited him.

Has Mark's book changed over time?

How different is Mark's original book from the book that we have today?

We don't have Mark's original to compare with the book we call Mark's Gospel. This is normal for ancient documents, since the original copy would have been written on material such as papyrus or parchment, which would eventually rot away.

For this reason historians assess the reliability of copies of an original by asking the following questions:

- How old are the copies?
- How much time has elapsed between the writing of the original document and the production of the copies that now exist?
- How many copies have been found?

The table below answers these questions for three widely-trusted historical works, and compares them with the New Testament (including Mark's Gospel).

As the table shows, the oldest surviving copies of Mark were produced 240 years after his original (a comparatively short time) and an astonishing 14,000 copies exist today. So we can have great confidence that what we read is what Mark wrote.

For more detail, *Can I Really Trust The Bible?* by Barry Cooper is a short, easy read.

	Date of original document	Date of oldest surviving copy	Approximate time between original and oldest surviving copy	Number of ancient copies in existence today
THUCYDIDES' HISTORY OF THE PELOPONNESIAN WAR	c. 431–400 BC	AD 900 plus a few late 1st-century fragments	1,300 years	73
CAESAR'S GALLIC WAR	c. 58–50 BC	AD 825	875 years	10
TACITUS' HISTORIES AND ANNALS	c. AD 98–108	c. AD 850	750 years	2
THE WHOLE NEW TESTAMENT	AD 40–100	AD 350	310 years	14,000 (approx 5,000 Greek; 8,000 Latin; 1,000 in other languages)
(MARK'S GOSPEL)	(AD 60–65)	(3rd century)	(240 years or less)	

MAP OF PLACES IN
MARK'S GOSPEL

Judy = Provident Village at Creekside
Hunter   Suite 120, 4838 S Cobb Drive
    Charlotte Hill   Smyrna, GA. 30080

                    (802) 356-1765
                    Judithbhunter@gmail.com

KEEP EXPLORING...

The *Christianity Explored* website (www.christianityexplored.org) helps you to keep exploring Jesus' life and message in your own way, at your own pace. It features:

- videos giving answers to tough questions.
- a visual outline explaining what Christianity is all about.
- real-life stories from people who've started to follow Jesus.